The Message 108

A Playbook to Manifesting & Achieving What Your Heart Desires

Charlotte Crumley Arrington

Written By: Charlotte Crumley Arrington

© 2021

ALL RIGHTS RESERVED. No part of this book may be reproduced in any written, electronic, recording, or photocopying without written permission of the publisher or author. The exception would be in the case of brief quotations embodied in the critical articles or reviews and pages where permission is specifically granted by the publisher or author.

LGEAL DISCLAIMER. Although the author has made every effort to ensure that the information in this book was correct at press time, the author do not assume and hereby disclaim any liability to any party for any loss, damage, or disruption caused by errors or omissions, whether such errors or omissions result from negligence, accident, or any other cause.

Published By: Pen Legacy, LLC

Cover & Formatting By: Tamika Ink

Edited By: Carla M. Dean of U Can Mark My Word

Library of Congress Cataloging – in- Publication Data has been applied for.

ISBN: 9781737012047

PRINTED IN THE UNITED STATES OF AMERICA.

Table of Content

Introduction 1

Change Your Message, Live Your Life 4

The Reward Comes From Blessing Others 13

Miracles Do Happen 24

Your Dreams Matter, Give Them Life 34

Humbleness Is Godly 46

Gratitude Is The Key To Success 55

Your Belief Dictates Your Destiny 66

The Power Of Manifestation 76

Congratulations .... **Error! Bookmark not defined.**

About The Author 94

Introduction

Congratulations! If you are reading this book, you have made the conscious decision to manifest greater and achieve everything your heart desires. My name is Charlotte Crumley Arrington, and I will be your coach as you embark on your journey. I am a motivational speaker, life coach, and businesswoman who is extremely passionate about encouraging people to do what God has called them to do and teaching tangible skills and scripture to make it happen.

Because I believed in my dream, I received my Bachelor of Art in Speech Communications from Howard University. I furthered my acumen for speaking by becoming a certified Speech and Debate Teacher. In addition, my education has afforded me the opportunity to use my communication and speaking gifts amongst some of the world's most influential people and major corporations. While working with a private jet company, I served the White House Press Corps, NBA, NHL, MLB, MLS, A-list celebrities, presidents, and national dignitaries. I have also served as the opening act for comedy shows starring Steve Harvey, Dave Chappelle, and Tommy Davidson. Lastly, I have worked with the NBA, NHL, and MLB as a team motivator. These experiences have given me the desire to serve YOU! It is time to share my knowledge, rewards, and gift with you. I've realized I need to focus on reaching the masses instead of those who already possess the expertise and indirectly share their space with me. For those expecting miracles, it is time for me to help them gain the faith, strength, and guidance they need. I am here to help you believe that your dreams matter. Your life requires more of your presence, and your faith needs to be reborn.

I will provide you with personal accounts, spiritual guidance, practical tools, and coaching advice to inspire you to believe in the beauty of your dreams. In addition, this book will serve as a playbook on how to expect, pray, and receive what you desire, just like I have in my life. Nothing in my life happened out of sheer fate; it was all ordained and orchestrated by my beliefs and God's answers. It is my hope that the chapters within this book will provide the same success for you. As you turn these pages, please know that you are reading the testimony and knowledge of someone who lived and is still living her dreams out loud. I have learned how to position myself to be the message that serves others.

The explanation for the title is simple. *The Message* is to do what God put you here to do. The number *108* is a spiritual number that represents the manifestation of your dreams. So, if you are ready to be served, let us begin your coaching journey. If you need anything along the way, feel free to contact me personally so I can motivate, inspire, or answer any questions to help you heal what is blocking the desires of your heart.

CHARLOTTE CRUMLEY ARRINGTON

Change Your Message, Live Your Life

Before we get into this book's message, can we agree that your mindset is 100% the blame for why you make certain choices, remain in situations that no longer serve you, and accept things that cannot elevate you? What you told yourself over the years has either paralyzed you into thinking life is supposed to be this way, or it motivates you to achieve more because you know you deserve it. Your mind is the vessel that controls your action muscle — embedding the attitudes, attributes, emotions, values, and feelings you use to live life. For instance, when something happens that you do not like, you typically respond based on your thoughts and feelings about the situation. Some people's first instinct is to react with an attitude and get defensive. Others will back away so as not to elevate drama, and a few will either handle the situation silently or entirely ignore it. Regardless of how you decide to attack a situation, to have a better outcome, we must understand how to change the way we think.

When it comes to understanding how to change your mindset, we must examine the two types: fixed mindset vs. growth mindset.

- Fixed Mindset ~ people who believe their qualities are inborn, fixed, and unchangeable.
- Growth Mindset ~ people who believe their abilities can be developed and strengthened through commitment and hard work.

As you can see, the biggest difference between the two types is how you believe in yourself and your ability to grow. Even though these mindsets can be created by our parents projecting their beliefs and fears onto us, we have the power to adjust our lives to fit our thoughts, needs, and desires. For example, have you ever seen a child who was overly concerned with being judged or who feared they might not live up to their parents' expectations? Having this kind of mindset, how do you think this child's life could end up? The amount of pressure alone could have this child thinking they have no control over their life or that nothing they ever do is good enough. Can anyone relate? How many of you are more concerned with others' expectations of you than your own happiness? If not adjusted, a fixed mindset will lead anyone down a negative path from the emotions and feelings it creates. Those with fixed mindsets are constantly seeking validation — living a life trying to please everyone. Again, am I speaking to you? Let me tell you, that was an exhausting life. Half of the time, I did not even know if I would achieve my dreams. I was simply going with the flow while believing and hoping for the best.

However, as I focused on my dreams becoming a reality, I developed more into a growth mindset. In this mindset, I found the power and peace to accept my need for personal growth, happiness, freedom, and love. I became clear on what I wanted, and I took proactive steps to receive it. I started exploring new things and people by networking with those who were outside of my comfort zone. I embraced new experiences and enjoyed challenges to grow past what I once thought was impossible. I started seeing mistakes and errors as learning lessons, and I stopped at nothing to correct them in the most beneficial way for me. As my belief in myself changed, so did my life. It was like I became unstoppable, and everything I once prayed for finally came true.

So, as you see, it wasn't until I started owning my life that I was able to grow my mindset and create the life I wanted. Ask yourself, do you own your life, or are you renting space out and keep settling for less? If you are looking to celebrate life and relieve stress, you must understand your mindset. How you think and believe is not only affecting your results but also costing you freedom. The following is a series of statements for you to agree or disagree with to better understand how you think. Some are based on a fixed mindset, and others are a growth mindset.

1. You hide your flaws so you are not judged or labeled a failure.

2. Your flaws are just a TO-DO list of things to improve.

3. You stick with what you know to keep up your confidence.

4. You keep up your confidence by constantly pushing into the unfamiliar to make sure you are always learning.

5. You commit to mastering valuable skills regardless of mood, knowing passion and purpose come from doing great work, which comes from expertise and experience.

6. Failures define you.

7. Failures are temporary setbacks.

8. You believe if you are romantically compatible with someone, you should share all of each other's views, and everything should just come naturally.

9. You believe a lasting relationship comes from effort and working through inevitable differences.

10. It is all about the outcome. If you fail, you think all effort was wasted.

11. It is all about the process, so the outcome hardly matters.

How do you think you did? Below are the statements with what kind of mindset they are:

1. You hide your flaws so you are not judged or labeled a failure. (Fixed)

2. Your flaws are just a TO-DO list of things to improve. (Growth)

3. You stick with what you know to keep up your confidence. (Fixed)

4. You keep up your confidence by constantly pushing into the unfamiliar to make sure you are always learning. (Growth)

5. You commit to mastering valuable skills regardless of mood, knowing passion and purpose come from doing great work, which comes from expertise and experience. (Growth)

6. Failures define you. (Fixed)

7. Failures are temporary setbacks. (Growth)

8. You believe if you are romantically compatible with someone, you should share all of each other's views, and everything should just come naturally. (Fixed)

9. You believe a lasting relationship comes from effort and working through inevitable differences. (Growth)

10. It is all about the outcome. If you fail, you think all effort was wasted. (Fixed)

11. It is all about the process, so the outcome hardly matters. (Growth)

Do you have a growth mindset or a fixed one? Do you have a mixture of both? Being clear on how you think will help you move through the rest of this book and your journey through life. Having a growth mindset is the key that separates winners from losers and entrepreneurs from millionaires. How hard are you willing to fight for what you want? Do you see your competitor as competition or a potential partner? Do you believe you are worthy of what you ask for? When you change your mindset, you change your life. I am profoundly grateful that I was able to change from a mindset of settling to a mindset of making everything achievable that I once thought was impossible. I took all the stones and heartbreaks thrown at me and created a queendom that now rewards me. Are you ready to transition from fixed to growth? Are you ready to believe and watch the universe manifest it for you? Here are seven ways I developed a growth mindset while transforming my life:

THE MESSAGE 108

1. Be willing to learn something daily.
2. Understand that perseverance is key.
3. Embrace challenges.
4. Develop a sense of personal responsibility.
5. Appreciate failure.
6. Accept constructive criticism.
7. Learn how to celebrate others with no motive.

As you go through shifting your mindset to accept life for what it is, only then will you begin to see it is not the end of the world when shifts happen. Sometimes shifts come to change the narrative or give us an advantage to win faster or more effectively. Stop looking at the glass as half full, and see it as always being full because you now have something of value to add to it. You are responsible for your life. No matter the disruption or damage in your path, you are given another chance to get it right every day you wake up. It is time for you to commit to a new life — a life devoted to who you are and who you are becoming. Author, public speaker, life coach, and philanthropist Tony Robbins once said, "If you want lasting change, you've got to give up this idea of 'trying something.' You've got to decide you're going to commit-to-mastery." It is time to quit "trying" and go for it. As I stated before, it is not easy. It took me multiple lessons before I got it right, but now, I live according to my own rules.

Are you ready to break every chain? Are you committed to yourself enough to know you deserve greatness? When you change your mindset, you change your life, and in doing that, it prevents the shifts formed against you from prospering. By creating a growth mindset, you'll get ahead of the storm and be able to see the storm before it lands.

The Reward Comes From Blessing Others

"Every man according as he purposeth in his heart, so let him give; not grudgingly, or of necessity: for God loveth a cheerful giver." ~ **2 Corinthians 9:7 (KJV)**

If you have attended a Baptist or Evangelist church, you may have heard this spoken to the congregation to encourage everyone to tithe or support the church's ministries. However, we can also associate this scripture with our lives in regards to how we can prepare ourselves to receive the blessings and abundance of God. Then there is **Galatians 6:7 (KJV),** which reminds us, *"Be not deceived; God is not mocked: for whatsoever a man soweth, that shall he also reap."* Between each scripture, God sets the tone that we get what we give to the world, the universe, and others. How many of you know that this is the first play needed to move in your abundance or getting your just due in life?

Before we dive into this, let me be the first to admit that I have not always been on point when it comes to giving in abundance or offering what I do not have. I will not say I was selfish, but at times, I felt people needed to carry their own weight. How many of you can relate? I mean, I have worked hard for what I have, and not so I can just give it away to those who may not be working hard enough or long enough, in my opinion. Then again, who am I to judge a person's work ethic? Do I know the circumstances concerning that person's story or struggle? Were they afforded the same opportunities? Without fully understanding someone's journey, how can I judge their lack and deny my ability to serve?

At the time, I did not understand that God blesses those He deems righteous enough to serve others. Some of our blessings are not meant to be kept to ourselves. Instead, they are to be shared with others to bring them to Him through Christ or make their crooked paths straight. We do not always know where our blessings come from, but we are quick to share what we acquire on social media. Just think how blessed you would be if you shared your blessing with someone personally before you ran to announce it to the world? Think of it this way: **God Blesses You + You Bless Others = Your Blessings Increase in Abundance.** It is no different than the circle of life; your blessings grow the more you bless others and share your gifts, especially if the gift is from God.

God blesses you so that you serve as his mouthpiece to bring more souls to him. Your testimony or success is by His grace, thus causing you to share His goodness, not your greatness. Are you tracking with me? You must understand that to be blessed, you must first be a blessing to others. *God Loves a Cheerful Giver* is more than a chant we say in church prior to paying our tithes and offerings in church. It is a lifestyle.

Now, I know you may be saying, "Charlotte, I don't have money or much to give, so how does someone like me receive the blessings I am praying for?" I am happy you asked because I, too, used to think my blessing was contingent upon how much money I could give when someone needed financial help. But can I tell you, money is the *key* to your blessing. Money is not connected to your blessing. Nowhere in the Bible does it say God loves a cheerful giver of *money*. I have yet to find that money is the gateway to answered prayers. When God refers to someone being a "cheerful giver", he is simply requesting you to give or share what he has blessed you with. For some, that can be money, but for others, it can be time, expertise, knowledge, support, love, friendship, or anything that stands in the gap of what that person needs. Some people need your support, nothing more. Others may need your knowledge and desire to sit at your feet to learn your wisdom; that can be your blessing to them. How you show up for them can be the blessing that awards you a prayer answered.

Whatever God has blessed you with, share it. What are you doing with all that you have right now anyway? Even though you have paid in some form to receive what you possess, sharing an ounce of it will cost you how much? Think how much better this world would be if we all shared just 1% of what we know. How much happier could we all be? How successful could we all be? How much struggle or pain could we prevent?

Before we move on, let's go deeper. Why don't we want to share our blessings with others? What has held you back from being the blessing to someone else when a blessing has saved you? With a pure heart and honesty, please answer the following questions that I have provided so you can face your issue and gain an understanding of why you are not being blessed the way you desire. Remember, we cannot heal what we cannot address.

What was I taught as a child as it relates to sharing?

_____
_____
_____
_____
_____
_____
_____

Am I afraid that people will take what I have prayed to receive if I share too much?

_____
_____
_____
_____
_____
_____

Do I believe God will replenish my cup if I give away all that I have?

Outside of money, what else can I offer others to help position them for a better life?

What have you learned about yourself? Are you shocked? Surprised? Many people do not realize that their current behaviors are a result of what they learned as a child or the mindset they adopted in their adulthood. Now that you know what is standing in the way of your abundant blessings, I challenge you to pray for growth so you can increase your value while serving others. Allow me to remind you that blessing others with an expectation of being blessed is a sure way to block your blessing.

Luke 6:35 (NASB) reminds us, *"But love your enemies, and do good, and lend, expecting nothing in return; and your reward will be great, and you will be sons of the Most High; for He Himself is kind to ungrateful and evil men."* Even though this scripture speaks of enemies, I want you to use the part that says "do good, and lend, expecting nothing in return; and your reward will be great" as your vessel to stay encouraged. Blessings with expectations will not only lead to you being disappointed, but it will also push you away from God's grace. Living with a sense of expectation or entitlement is how many of us lose what we worked so hard for — because we lose the feeling of humility or humbleness. However, let me remind you that just as fast as God can giveth, he can also take away. There is a reason and lesson behind everything you go through; nothing is by circumstance.

I often tell people, the way you treat others will be the way God treats you. If you get upset because your friend did not sacrifice for you the way you sacrificed for her, you must ask yourself whether you were giving from the heart or a place of expectation. When you expect something in return, you are setting yourself up for failure and a life of loneliness because you will cut off everyone. Remember, God blessed you with a gift that he did not bless others with — being uniquely you. That is *your* superpower. Thus, you will never get *you* back from anyone. If God blessed everyone to be like you, what would make you stand out? So right here, right now, let us bury the concept of expectation or entitlement and lean on the understanding that when you bless others, it will come back to you tenfold. Also, your blessing doesn't always come back from the person you served. It may come back in the form of success, a promotion, a relationship, an opportunity, or a blessing for your spouse, child, or family member. The result of your blessings does not always have to come back to you; it can serve those you have prayed for. You are a vessel that serves and saves. There cannot be an expectation attached to that.

Always remember, God created the universe for us to take care of each other. If you assist and support someone else, it will come back to you. I know God will return the blessing to myself or my children and grandchildren throughout my journey of being a blessing to others. My spirit of giving is never about my come-up but my ability to uplift the next person by motivating them to be happy, follow their dreams, and become who they desire. In addition, you never know who you are assigned to when it comes to your blessing. You might be assigned a waitress who will become the next chief operating officer of her own business or the next president. You never know who needs your testimony, your experience, and your story. Did you know your growth could be in your ability just to have a conversation? You reap what you sow! You give what you get. The more you serve and share, the more the universe will serve and share back to your address. Get out of your own way by thinking you are holding someone else back by withholding information when, in return, you are only blocking yourself. God loves a cheerful giver, so never forget who gave you!

Additional Scriptures:

- Proverbs 16:24 — Pleasant words are a honeycomb, sweet to the soul and healing to the bones.
- Proverbs 15:30 — A cheerful look brings joy to the heart and good news gives health to the bones.

- Proverbs 22:1 — A good name is more desirable than great riches: to be esteemed is better than silver or gold.

The Message 108 Coaching Tips

Be a Blessing. If you see a need and something within you is telling you to help, give. Do it and do not delay. If a kind word pops into your head for someone, say it. If someone asks you to do them a favor and you can do it, do it. If someone is asking for help and you can help them, help them. Volunteer someplace, using the gifts God has given you.

What You Give is What You Get. Whatever you give, you're going to get it back. For example, if you give love, you will get love back. If you give hate, you will get hate back. If you give candy, you will get candy back. If you give money, you will get money back. So, always be conscious of what you are giving because what you give is what you get. The good news about giving is that it's generational. By blessing someone today, it may be returned with your children, grandchildren, etc.

Be a Cheerful Giver. Only give if you feel good about it. When you give something, make sure your heart is in it, and you are not looking for anything in return. Give because you want to and not because you have to. When you give because you want to make a positive difference, your giving will come back to you. When you give, it is between you, the recipient, and God. There is no need for you to tell everyone what you did. God sees and knows if your heart is pure. Give with no expectations. Giving selfishly means expecting something in return. Actually, if you look to receive back what you give, that's considered borrowing. You will not be blessed if that's your way of thinking regarding giving to others.

CHARLOTTE CRUMLEY ARRINGTON

Miracles Do Happen

While in college, I struggled with paying tuition and buying books, all while being a mother of twins and having a baby on the way. I knew something had to give, but I remained hopeful that something would turn around to allow me to finish the program and secure my degree. So, one day, I decided to visit the financial aid office on campus to seek assistance. I spent the entire day going from office to office only to be told, "Sorry, there is nothing we can do for you." After being denied for five hours, I left discouraged and cried all the way home. Mentally, I was spent. How could there be no help for me? Especially since my grades were good.

As I fell deeper into my thoughts of self-pity, I recalled attending a luncheon hosted by my sorority Zeta Phi Beta Incorporated. A reporter for the White House Corps was the guest speaker. During her speech, she spoke about overcoming challenging situations. In all things, she expected a miracle for things to change, and they did! That's it! EXPECT A MIRACLE! In that moment, I said to myself, "I'm going to the Dean's office and ask for a scholarship." And that's exactly what I did. I dried my eyes, then knocked on every door, looked under every stone, and asked everyone I could. As a result of my persistence, I received a scholarship that covered my last two years of college as long as I maintained a 3.0 grade point average. Not only did I maintain that requirement, but I excelled to receive a 4.0 grade point average and obtained the President's Scholarship the following year, which afforded me enough money to pay for my children's pre-school tuition on Howard's campus.

When you give yourself permission to expect a miracle, you are permitting yourself to believe there is more for you. There is hope left. All is not lost. Just think what could have happened if I succumbed to my pity in that car and went home. I would have had to drop out of college and try to make it with the tools I had that probably would have kept me stuck. But, my hope led me back to the campus.

I know many of you probably do not believe in miracles and lean more on faith-based thinking and movement. That is fine. However, allow me to enlighten you on how miracles are also a positive attribute when living the life you want. According to Merriam-Webster Dictionary, the definition of "miracle" is,

- an extraordinary event manifesting divine intervention in human affairs
- an extremely outstanding or unusual event, thing, or accomplishment
- a divinely natural phenomenon experienced humanly as the fulfillment of spiritual law.

By expecting miracles, you are giving yourself permission to win. You are expecting things to work for your good and in your favor. You are positioning yourself to receive what you want. Miracles are those little things that show up when we least expect them and at the point where we feel all hope is gone. Miracles remind us that there is always light at the end of the tunnel if we only believe. We know there is more for us, so we expect greater. We know God has a plan for our journey, so we expect grace and favor. Knowing that you will receive more is an understanding of how God will show up at any given moment to bless you with what you need.

Some of you may say that having expectations is the same as having faith. When you expect a miracle, you are leaning on your faith in knowing that God will make a way for you. And you are absolutely right! When we expect a miracle, we are ultimately evoking faith, spirituality, and a belief that something greater than ourselves will intercede on our behalf and help elicit positive changes in our life. Expecting a miracle is the spiritual belief that your God is able to do exceedingly abundantly above all things that we ask. Faith is the spiritual side that provides you the strength and fuel to ignite that expectation.

Hebrew 11:1, KJV tells us, *"Now faith is the substance of things hoped for, the evidence of things not seen."* Carl Sagan, the late and noted author, once said, "Faith is believing in something in the absence of evidence." For many, this is hard because many of us need to physically see things with our own eyes to believe it exists. How many of you are afraid to leap toward your success because you do not have a clear map showing you when you will acquire your millions or how long it will take to reach your final destination? Some of you are waiting for evidence and instructions from others, which no one can truly provide. Everyone's journey is different, and everyone's knowledge prior to jumping gives them a unique parachute to survive longer in the sky.

So, before you expect a miracle, ask yourself how strong is your faith. Do you need a life manual before taking that leap? What is shaky in your spirit that makes you hesitant about expecting a miracle? Take a pulse check. Get clear on what is preventing you from asking for help instead of sitting alone crying in despair. How many of you threw in the towel too soon? Do you have enough faith to pull the towel back and try again?

Answer the following questions to face your reality so you can heal forward.

I often do not trust faith because I am afraid of…

_____
_____
_____
_____
_____
_____

What proof am I waiting for that is preventing me from becoming who I desire to be?

What tools do I need to pull back to win at this thing called life?

What do I need help with, and who can I ask?

_____
_____
_____
_____
_____
_____
_____
_____

As you see, faith is the spiritual belief behind expecting a miracle, but you must live expecting that God and good are on your side. God does not want you to live in despair or a state of depression, leading you to believe all hope is gone for you and your dreams. Your mindset requires you to believe that you are deserving of whatever you want in life. You are worthy of obtaining a scholarship, a promotion, getting married, relocating, or whatever your heart desires. When you know deep down inside that God has you, you can expect to experience a miracle, greater blessings, and rewards.

Your Scripture:

- Mark 11:22-24 — "Have faith in God," Jesus answered. "Truly I tell you, if anyone says to this mountain, 'Go, throw yourself into the sea,' and does not doubt in their heart but believes that what they say will happen, it will be done for them. Therefore I tell you, whatever you ask for in prayer, believe that you have received it, and it will be yours."
- John 4:48 — "So Jesus said to him, "Unless you see signs and wonders you will not believe."
- 1 Corinthians 13:13 — "So now **faith**, **hope**, and love abide, these three; but the greatest of these is love."

The Message 108 Coaching Tips

Do You Believe? You have to believe that what you see in your mind and feel in your soul and spirit will happen. No matter what the outside circumstances look like, you have to believe you will succeed. What you see as your success will happen for you. Regardless of what you may need and do not have, or what seems impossible, you have to believe. That is when the power of the miracle gets stronger.

Where is Your Faith? You have to have faith the size of a mustard seed, which is the smallest of all seeds. It may seem impossible for a mustard seed to host beautiful birds once it becomes a tree or be enough to feed a nation. Your dreams may seem just as impossible. When you start experiencing feelings of self-doubt, you must hold on to your faith. Your faith will allow you to see beyond what's in front of your eyes. Faith will allow you to stay focused on the future while making preparations in the present; faith will allow you to believe in a better outcome when you feel like giving up. You have to practice these principles, though. When things are going good, give thanks for answered prayers. When times are trying, give thanks for what your faith has brought you through. At all times, give thanks and maintain your faith.

Follow the Rule of Seek, Knock, Ask. Needing a miracle is when you have done everything in your power to make the thing that you need to happen a reality. When we **ask**, we **ask** with faith — believing God's promises are true and that we are not hurting ourselves or anyone else by our asking. When we **seek**, we **seek** possible answers with eyes of faith, meaning we keep our eyes on the prize. In other words, we are seeking God's promises to us. When we **knock**, we take a risk and step out on faith by pursuing opportunities discovered during the **seeking** phase. We make calls, knock on doors, and seek wisdom. These are the steps that make miracles happen.

You Must Have Courage. It takes a lot of courage to believe in the gifts that God has given you. Once you recognize you have something special, it takes courage to fully embrace that gift and make it a way of life for you. It takes courage because you need to be able to keep going when not only self-doubt but external doubt creeps upon you. And unfortunately, it will come. It takes courage to confess out loud, "Yes, I am going to do this. Yes, this is my dream. Yes, this is who I am, and yes, this is who I am going to become." Whatever you do, be courageous and stay focused on achieving your dreams.

CHARLOTTE CRUMLEY ARRINGTON

Your Dreams Matter, Give Them Life

I have always been one to believe in myself and what I wanted to achieve in life. I am gifted with the power of motivating others because I first learned the importance of motivating myself. My first dream was to become a flight attendant because I thought it would afford me a lifestyle of excitement, travel, and encouraging others. However, after giving my candidacy speech for president at Dana Jr. High School, that feeling made me intrigued about becoming a speaker. By the way, my speech led to me winning, and I became the best student body president ever!

The feeling I experienced made me pursue a degree in communications at Howard University. While attending Howard, I discovered that the message is the information, conversation, and knowledge that God intended for us to share with others. Our testimonies serve as confirmation of how God can show up and show out in your life. Thus, this made me want to become a motivational speaker. With all I had been through, I wanted to be the example of God's miracles, grace, and mercy. So, my dream of speaking and being a flight attendant was birthed, and after graduating college, I was able to do both.

What was your initial dream of who you wanted to be or what you wanted to have in your life? Did any of your dreams come true for you? Let's do a pulse check. Go back to who you desired to be and work your way to the present. Clearly understand who you wanted to be, what got in the way, and how you can still make that dream come true. Answer the following questions about who you desired to become.

When I was a child, I dreamed of having a lifestyle where I was…

_____
_____
_____
_____

CHARLOTTE CRUMLEY ARRINGTON

_____
_____
_____
_____

My dreams were important to me as a child because they gave me...

_____
_____
_____
_____
_____
_____
_____
_____

Unfortunately, my dreams were halted because...

_____
_____
_____
_____
_____
_____
_____
_____

THE MESSAGE 108

If I haven't fulfilled my dreams yet, do I still believe in myself enough to make them come true?

_____
_____
_____
_____
_____
_____
_____

Am I willing to do the work (i.e., get training, obtain a degree, volunteer to gain experience, partner with others) to make my dreams come true? If yes, who can help me?

_____
_____
_____
_____
_____
_____
_____

I have accomplished most of my dreams, but I still have a desire to…

_____
_____
_____
_____
_____
_____
_____
_____

Now ask yourself if you have achieved your dreams. When did you stop working towards your dreams, or why did you have to adjust them? Helping you to achieve your dreams is my most important mission. As someone who pursued her dreams and accomplished them, I can attest that it is a breathtaking experience to fulfill those dreams you had as a child. Saying "YES" to yourself is the most humbling and rewarding gift on earth. I want that for you, but do you want it for yourself? Are you standing firm in your faith and expecting a miracle that your dream will come true for you?

My dreams came true for me after graduating from college. I became a First-Class Flight Attendant with

American Airlines, and that position led me to become a Lead Flight Attendant for a charter company. While in the position with the charter company, I birthed my dream of becoming a motivational speaker. This position allowed me the opportunity to motivate and communicate with professional sports teams and their players. How amazing is that! It did not hit me that I was living my wildest dreams until one day, while taking a flight with team players, I realized the plane was where the real locker room talk went down. I thought my motivating speeches to them would take place within the stadium or in the locker room. Instead, it mostly happened when we were all on the plane; it is where they could be themselves. Whether they were unwinding from a big victory or a salty loss, I was there to listen, encourage, support, and motivate. The motivational conversations I had with them ended up creating lasting friendships.

For example, one night before the Blackhawks won the Stanley Cup against the Philadelphia Flyers, one of the players invited me to his hotel room to hang out. I found his request to be random and weird since most of our conversations occurred on the plane whenever I was serving him or when he came back to the galley to say hello. However, on this particular evening, I saw this as an assignment from God to serve. When I arrived, he asked, "Can we talk?" Lo and behold, he just wanted someone to watch television with and to listen to him. We spent the evening watching our favorite shows and engaging in great conversation about the job, his role, and the stresses that came with it. At that moment, I learned that being a professional sports player on the road is often lonely. Some genuinely need a good friend — someone to listen and be there with them. As he prepared to retire for the night, he thanked me for keeping him company and then gave me one hundred dollars for cab fare, which was a blessing because I only had enough money to get there. When I got back to my hotel, my heart was full of delight that my gift was being used. I was in a good space to be available to provide positive energy and calmness.

The next night, the team won the Stanley Cup. How sweet! After we flew back to Chicago, the team threw a private party. During the party, the player who I had visited at the hotel made sure he introduced me to his mother and girlfriend and shared the good deed I had done for him. It was a little thing to them, but to me, it was my opportunity to share God's word, grace, and peace with him.

THE MESSAGE 108

Then there was another time when the Boston Celtics lost the championship to the Miami Heat. The star player did not want to get on the plane. As he was refusing, I heard God's voice tell me to give him a message. Being obedient, I got off the plane, sat next to him on the stairs, and delivered the message God had put into my spirit for him. After a few minutes, I asked him, "Are you ready to get on the plane now?" He replied, "Yes." After returning home to Boston, the team received a hero's welcome from their fans.

These two situations solidified my purpose; I knew who I was supposed to be. I had a way of communicating that offered support and guidance to help others face their fears and reach their goals. For many who I have helped, fear has been the #1 reason they have not achieved their dreams. For some, it is the fear of losing, failing, being criticized, lack of support, or ending relationships. Fear will kill any dream. How has being afraid affected your ability to achieve your dreams? For others, it is the fear of not being good enough, worthy enough, or more qualified than others. Who do you measure yourself up against? Use the following six tactics to combat fear when it begins to invade your spirit:

- ➢ Stop trying to figure things out by yourself.
- ➢ Be honest about how you feel and give it a voice.
- ➢ Be okay with some things being out of your control.
- ➢ Be conscious of your intentions.
- ➢ Focus on positive thoughts.
- ➢ Train your brain to stop the fear response.

We have to understand that we can do all things when we stop trying to execute them alone. The tactics I mentioned are great to apply when facing your fears. The moment you start facing your fears will be the turning point in your life and the beginning of pursuing your dreams. So, use these ideas to jumpstart your progress, not avoid it.

Your Scriptures:

- Proverbs 16:3 — "Commit to the Lord whatever you do and your plans will succeed."
- Proverbs 3:5-6 — "Trust in the Lord with all your heart and lean not on your only understanding; in all your ways submit to him and he will make your path straight."
- Jeremiah 29:11 — "For I know the plans I have for you," declares the Lord, "plans to prosper you

and not to harm you, plans to give you hope and a future."

The Message 108 Coaching Tips

Believe It. Your gift was planted in you when you were born; it is a part of your spirit. You have to believe in that gift. You will know it is real if it gives you that satisfied feeling you get after eating a good meal. That is how living your dream will feel, like eating a delicious pot of gumbo, a Philly cheesesteak, a carne asada burrito, sushi or whatever is your favorite dish. When you indulge in good food, you feel as though all is well in the world. You have to carry this feeling with you throughout whatever you go through. Believe in your gift even if no one else believes in you. It starts with you. If you do not believe in yourself, no one else will.

Speak on it. Share your dream with people who can help you. Call yourself who you want to be. Regardless of what positions I held at my jobs, I always called myself a motivational speaker. You have to let people know what you do, so they will contact you when they need your services. Study your craft, volunteer your time, and use your craft to be a blessing to others. It may sound or feel strange to hear yourself professing to do something you are not doing or being someone you are not yet. However, you will eventually get to the point where you are who you claimed to be and doing what you said you would do. You just have to believe it in your spirit. Do not be distracted by people who try to deter you from your dreams by telling you that you cannot do something or that it is not a good idea. God gave us all gifts, and they are to be used. Your gift may just bless a nation. Your gift is what makes you unique from everyone else. So, have courage and tell people about your services. Speak on it, and don't let anyone silence you.

Trust It. Trust in your dream and trust that you will receive what you need to make your dream a reality. For me, I knew if I earned a degree in Communications, I would be more knowledgeable about my subject, and it would give me more credibility. Trust yourself with your gift and understand it. Trust the process of educating yourself and learning your craft. Trust that opportunities will happen as you train and prepare yourself to work in your gift. Trust yourself to get the job done. The more you trust yourself to do these things, the stronger your gift will be and the more trust you will have in the next opportunity.

Education. Make sure you educate yourself about your dream, meaning studying and doing research about the things that are in direct relation to your goals. There is a course for whatever plan you have. When I wanted to become a flight attendant, I took classes in that field at my local community college. Once I applied for the position, I knew what to expect versus someone who did not take the time to educate themselves. As a result, I was offered a job with each airline for which I applied. Since I wanted to become a motivational speaker, I also went to college to obtain a degree in Communications. By educating yourself about your gift, you will feel more secure in performing your duties and will become an expert in the field. Educating yourself is one of your best investments. The more educated you are in your field, the more credibility you will have, and the more doors will open for you. Not to mention, convincing someone to trust you and your gifts will be a little easier.

Humbleness Is Godly

Outside of being a blessing to others, being humble is your second play to winning success. For some people, not practicing humility has cost them their freedom, wealth, relationships, and success. Just because God blesses you with having something that others do not possess does not mean you have the right to be cocky, arrogant, or powerful. Blessings do not make you supreme over others. Nor does it mean you should expect people to bow down to you or stroke your ego because you made it, and they did not…yet. Yes, I said yet, because everyone will receive a chance at winning. Nobody will remain beneath you for long. Either they will rise up and surpass you, or you will lose ground and fall back down. Thus, humility is your friend.

To understand this concept, let's look at what it means in a spiritual sense. Godly humility is being comfortable with who you are in the Lord and therefore put others first. The picture of humility in the Bible is one of a strong person who loves others, not someone who is a wimp. Philippians 2:3 tells us, *"Do nothing out of selfish ambition or vain conceit, but in humility consider others better than yourselves."* In addition, humility is recognizing that you need God's help, knowing you cannot truly succeed in your own strength. It is thanking God for your talents and gifts and giving him credit for your accomplishments. How many of you brag and boast on social media about something you have achieved? Do you ever thank God for your ability to do the things that have resulted in your success? Have you thanked your parents for their teachings and wisdom? Or do you take all of the credit? Being humble is understanding where your gift comes from. It is giving God and others thanks first and then praising yourself on a job well done. Nobody can achieve greatness alone. For example,

- parents or grandparents teach us values and morals,
- teachers educate us on theory and concepts within many subjects,
- friends teach us social skills and how to interact with others effectively,

- spiritual mothers/fathers and leaders offer teachings and directions of God,
- best friends keep us in check and help us look at things from a different perspective,
- leaders set the bar and offer tips to climb the ladder of success, and
- coaches and counselors teach us how to maintain self-control in order to make better decisions.

After that breakdown of everyone who has helped you become the person you are today, how could you think the only person you should be thanking is yourself? Being humble is realizing that you are who you are because of the village that cared for and carried you to your highest potential. Now, I am not saying you have to give an Oscar acceptance speech every time you achieve something, but you must respect that you are not the only one responsible for being in the position you landed. Before we move on, take a minute and think of all the people who are responsible for where you are right now, whether good or bad. Some people did us wrong, but we can also give them thanks because their lessons taught us how to handle a situation better. Or the experience may have helped build our self-esteem. Yes, you have to protect yourself at all costs, but who has a stake in your blessings?

THE MESSAGE 108

Here is your chance to give your Oscar speech. Who would you like to thank?

CHARLOTTE CRUMLEY ARRINGTON

Being humble is giving others responsible for your success their roses while they are here or doing something in remembrance of them if they have left this branch of Zion. I have been blessed to receive everything I want and prayed for because I remain humble. I am not afraid to give God praise and thank those who added to my greatness. I know for a fact that I could not have accomplished all that I have by myself. I am not afraid to ask for help, and I am humble enough to know I do not know it all. I am also comfortable enough in my skin to know when I am wrong or have done something out of line.

Can I share a secret with you? When it comes to being humble, one of the greatest rewards is you will always win no matter what. You may lose one opportunity, but knowing that something better is coming leaves you with a sense of being available. You are not always meant to win the first thing; sometimes, losing gives you the ability to win what God wants for you. This is because, as humans, we typically go with our instinct before consulting with God, then wonder why we are losing. Or God sets us up to lose so we can gain respect and patience for that which we seek. Thus, humility allows us to appreciate the process and respect what is ahead. When God sees this, only then can He and will He trust you with more.

You will usually be more successful when you practice what the Bible says about God and humility than if you are pushy or arrogant. When you are humble, you are likely to have more influence than when you fight abrasively. Even if you don't achieve the results you hoped for, you have the joy of having acted in a godly manner. When you understand the meaning of humility and put it into practice, you are a winner—even if you do not "win."

Your Scriptures:

- Luke 14:11 — "For all those who exalt themselves will be humbled and those who humble themselves will be exalted."
- Proverbs 19:20 — "Listen to advice and accept instruction, and in the end, you will be wise."
- James 4:6 — "But He gives a greater grace. Therefore, it says, 'God is opposed to the proud, but gives grace to the humble.'"

The Message 108 Coaching Tips

Be Quiet. Being humble can be as simple as being quiet and just listening. So many times, we want to be right during a conversation or argument that we do not listen to the other person. We already have our minds made up and will fight for our side to be heard. If we would be quiet and listen to the other person's side, we will see that we may have missed the point and be wrong after all. Just be quiet and wait for the other person or people to finish speaking, and I promise you will have their undivided attention. What you give is what you get.

Life is Short. Being right all of the time is exhausting. Life is too short for arguing with people about how right you are and always trying to be right. Sometimes we have to humble ourselves and let the other person be right. Life is meant to be peaceful, and you will not have any peace if you are fighting to be right all the time. The worst feeling in the world is when a loved one or friend dies, and the two of you were not speaking at the time of their death because you wanted to be right in a disagreement. Many people carry that guilt around for not mending that relationship before the person's demise because they could not humble themselves and admit they were wrong or that what they were arguing about did not matter. It is so much better to be humble if you will experience more peace and happy times.

Judging. This is one of the hardest principles to practice when it comes to being humble. We are quick to judge someone to make ourselves look or feel better. It is the worst thing you can do because you're inviting bad karma when you judge someone. If you're judging someone else's circumstances, there may come a day when you find yourself in that same predicament. Train yourself to be compassionate and nonjudgmental towards others and their problems. We are all guilty of judging others; it is a part of human nature. However, being judgmental is one of the biggest ways you can block your future blessings. Be part of the solution, not the problem.

No One is Perfect. No one is perfect, not even your mama. I can and will humbly speak for myself. As a mother of grown children, I know I could have done some things better, and it took a while for me to let go of the guilt. We strive to be perfect, and that is great. However, we are all going to fall short of the glory. What I have realized is that God designed it for parents not to be perfect. Think about it. Since our first interaction with people is our parents, if they are not perfect, then nobody is perfect, not even us. With that said, do not take it personally when someone does something wrong to you. We all make mistakes. Forgive them and keep it moving because one day, you will need forgiveness. I promise.

Gratitude Is the Key To Success

As we discussed in the previous chapter, giving thanks and praise to those who paved the way and made your road easier is essential to your success. I honestly believe it is our responsibility to give thanks for everything you have, everything you have lost, and everything that is forthcoming. In fact, gratitude may be one of the most overlooked tools we can access every day. Cultivating gratitude does not cost any money, and it certainly does not take much time, but the benefits are enormous.

If you are like me, you spend a lot of time asking God for more without fully appreciating and giving thanks for all that He has blessed you with already. At times, we ask God for things that He already provided us, but because it is not packaged how we want it, we pray for better and more. Let me remind you that God never gives us exactly what we want. He provides what you need to sustain. He is like a parent that only gives you what you need at the moment. When you show appreciation for what He has given, He will provide you with more, and the process grows as you show gratitude. We must remember not to be greedy or demanding because everything God provides is either a promise or a gift. Anything extra is grace and favor.

How have you shown your appreciation for what God has given you? How many times a day do you complain about your job and want to quit when there are over 10.1 million people unemployed in the United States? How many of you complain that your apartment is too small or your house is old when there is an estimated 553,742 people who are homeless. When is the last time you thanked God for having the ability to provide during a pandemic when so many are hurting? Having gratitude helps us level out our perspective and remain patient until we are better positioned to achieve more. Think back to when you were a child and eating dinner. When you asked for more food, did your parents pile more on your plate, or did they tell you to finish what you had first, and then you could get more if you were still hungry? It is the same with gratitude. You must enjoy and take in everything you have before you are blessed with more.

A spirit of gratitude and appreciation is an essential skill for *everyone* – young and old – to foster and develop! Gratitude promotes optimism and helps us create a more positive outlook. It lets us pause to reflect on the thing(s) we have in our life right now instead of always striving for more — the next goal, the new dress, the new car, house renovations, etc. Gratitude is simply cultivating a genuine appreciation for what we already have. Now, I am not saying settle for what you already have, but merely learn how to appreciate what you have before you leap to acquire more. This is what separates those filled with greed and lust from those blessed beyond measure. The Bible reminds us in Romans 8:28, ***"And we know that for those who love God all things work together for good, for those who are called according to his purpose."***

What things are you grateful for? Let us take inventory and examine everything we have in our lives yet may be taking for granted. What are you seeking but do not realize is within your reach? Answer the following questions to get a clear understanding of what you have, what you are taking for granted, and what you are still praying for without fully investing in yourself first.

I show my sense of gratitude by...

_____
_____
_____
_____
_____
_____
_____

I do not always show my gratitude because I feel as though I...

_____
_____
_____
_____
_____
_____
_____

I am personally responsible for my success and everything I have, so showing gratitude is something I do not do because...

_____
_____
_____
_____
_____
_____
_____

Knowing what I know now, I am willing to be grateful because I am ready to receive...

_____
_____
_____
_____
_____
_____
_____
_____

I can remember my ex-husband and I had friends who appeared to be more financially stable than us. At times,

I would get discouraged and question God, wondering why people around us were better off financially while we struggled to make ends meet. I compared our life to those around us, and it always made me feel as though we were inadequate or doing something wrong. I never considered their job positions and income brackets, financial sacrifices, or if they had a budget or financial advisor. I just knew they were better off, and I wanted more. I wanted the freedom they had, but after God chin-checked me, I was faced with a dose of reality. I had failed to look around our home and see all we had gained together in our marriage. I was putting so much stress, pressure, and expectations on us that I missed moments of gratefulness. In that moment, I put down my feelings, picked up my bible, and began giving thanks. It hit me that someone somewhere was crying out to God and praying for what we had. That was my turning point. I allowed myself the ability to sit in my grace and prepare for the more that God would provide in His time.

Proverbs 27:1 reminds us, *"Do not boast about tomorrow, for you do not know what a day may bring."*

In other words, recognize that we have God to thank for each day that we rise. We do not know what tomorrow will bring, so we should celebrate each day and live by honoring God in the gift of life that we often take for granted. Life as we know it can change in a blink of an eye, which should give us an even more powerful purpose to be grateful for the presence of today. We should rejoice in the moments of our gifts, talents, and the ability to provide today. When we change our perspective to focus on the present, we learn how to enjoy what we have and prepare for the more that is on the way. As you move forward to become one within your spirit of gratefulness, here are six ways to become grateful throughout your day:

- **Keep a Gratitude Journal.** Establish a daily practice in which you remind yourself of the gifts, grace, benefits, and good things you enjoy.
- **Remember the Bad.** To be grateful in your current state, remember the hard times you once experienced and how you overcame them.
- **Ask Yourself Three Questions.** Utilize the meditation technique, which involves reflecting on three questions: "What have I received from __?", "What have I given to __?" and "What troubles and difficulties have I caused?"

- **Come to Your Senses.** Through our senses—the ability to touch, see, smell, taste, and hear—we gain an appreciation of what it means to be human and of what an incredible miracle it is to be alive.
- **Watch Your Language.** Grateful people have a particular linguistic style that uses the language of gifts, givers, blessings, blessed, fortune, fortunate, and abundance. In gratitude, you should not focus on how inherently good you are but instead on the inherently good things others have done on your behalf.
- **Think Outside the Box.** If you want to make the most out of opportunities to flex your gratitude muscles, you must creatively look for new situations and circumstances for which to feel grateful.

After applying many gratitude techniques and leaning on God's word, I decided to be thankful for everything I had and become a blessing to others. Trust me, this mindset shift did not happen overnight, but now I smile and celebrate. I am penning this book with so much joy in my heart, knowing that God chose me to become the messenger. How many of you know someone who is living every single dream they have prayed for? How many of you know someone who has everything they want and asks for? The lyrics to "Amazing Grace" continue to play on my spirit — "Was blind, but now I see." I no longer measure my life against those around me, whether in reality or on social media. I am comfortable knowing I may not have everything life has to offer, but I also know there is someone somewhere praying for at least half of what I have.

We all have the ability and opportunity to cultivate gratitude. Take a few moments to focus on all you have rather than complain about all the things you think you deserve. Developing an "attitude of gratitude" is one of the simplest ways to improve your satisfaction with life.

Your Scriptures:

- James 1:2-4 — "Count it all joy, my brothers, when you meet trials of various kinds, for you know that the testing of your faith produces steadfastness. And let steadfastness have its full effect, that you may be perfect and complete, lacking in nothing."
- Philippians 4:6-7 — "Do not be anxious about anything, but in every situation, by prayer and petition, with thanksgiving, present your requests to God. And the peace of God, which

transcends all understanding, will guard your hearts and your minds in Christ Jesus."
- Hebrews 13:15-16 — "Through Jesus, therefore, let us continually offer to God a sacrifice of praise — the fruit of lips that openly profess his name. And do not forget to do good and to share with others, for with such sacrifices God is pleased."

The Message 108 Coaching Tips

Be Thankful. Be thankful for what you have. Most of us are always asking God for more instead of taking the time to be thankful for what we have. It's okay to want more, but if you are not thankful for what you already have, what you get later still will not be enough. We take for granted most of the things we have to be thankful for, such as our eyesight, hearing, and ability to walk. Once we start being more thankful for the little things in our life, God will give us the bigger things we want in life.

Share. Volunteer your time sharing your gift with others. This is the best way to determine if you are passionate about what you want to do. For example, if you like building things, volunteer for Habitat for Humanity. It will give you the opportunity to use your gift and be a blessing to someone else. If you like to sing, volunteer to sing at a friend's wedding or put on a show at a nursing home. It is also a way of giving gratitude because you are saying you are so grateful for your gift that you are willing to share it with others without expecting anything in return.

Your Belief Dictates Your Destiny

Merriam-Webster Dictionary defines belief as being "a state or habit of mind in which trust or confidence is placed in some person or thing." Another definition for belief is "conviction of the truth of some statement or the reality of some being or phenomenon especially when based on examination of evidence." Let's focus on the second definition: "the conviction of the truth." When it comes to your belief system, you must have a solid conviction that what you know to be true is law and valuable to your destiny. What do you have a strong belief about? When it comes to building a strong belief system, you must first understand what you believe in and how that thought process will affect your mindset, which in turn will affect your destiny (future). What you believe about yourself, your abilities, and your future will ultimately come true, but be careful because your thoughts can bring either good or bad karma your way.

Before we move forward, examine your beliefs and get clear on how you think about yourself, your current state, and your future. How we see ourselves will either give us permission to soar or settle. Many people will never live out the true potential of their lives because their beliefs will only allow them to go but so far. How many of you saw an amazing opportunity and immediately thought you should apply? But then, right before applying, your limiting beliefs step in, your self-sabotaging conversations begin in your head, and what you got excited about immediately becomes a distant memory. You decide not to pursue the opportunity even though you know it could get you one step closer to your dreams and goals. What are your beliefs? Let's take a moment and reflect on your current beliefs by answering the following questions:

What self-limiting beliefs have you convinced yourself to be true?

_____

_____

How did you gain your belief structure? Are they rooted in values, morals, family traditions, or personal experience?

Do you judge yourself based on your ability to achieve? Are you afraid to fail?

Are you operating your life on purpose or prevention?

What have your beliefs blocked you from achieving? What have you prayed for or are currently seeking now?

"You begin to fly when you let go of self-limiting beliefs and allow your mind and aspirations to rise to greater heights." ~ Brian Tracy

Are you flying? Your beliefs control your destiny because they are the imprint upon which the future is cast. Think about how you acquired your beliefs and whether they have changed over time. As you see from your answers, our beliefs are typically a product of the wisdom and teachings of our parents. I don't know about you, but a belief embedded in me was the "employee methodology" — graduate from high school, get a job, have a family, retire at retirement age, try to enjoy the remaining of your life, and then meet God on Judgment Day. How many of you are operating in that same belief? Securing a pension is more important than living a dream or traveling the world. With this new generation, they ignore that belief and have become committed to entrepreneurship and being the boss over their lives. They follow no rules or traditions except for the ones they create along the way. The painstaking hard work approach our parents were familiar with has been replaced with big ideas and innovation. The point

I wish to make is that we must upgrade our beliefs as our lives and the circumstances in our society change. The question is, are you willing to upgrade your beliefs?

Sadly, many people go to their grave having lived a less than optimal life and call it fate or destiny. We have far more choices about our life than we recognize. Therefore, we must be mindful whether we are choosing from a place of fear or a place of life. This is why getting our beliefs intact is essential. If our beliefs are flawed, we will choose accordingly and call it fate since we do not know better. We can be punishing ourselves without even knowing it. How many of you are currently doing this right now? How many of you are so convicted on your belief that you are standing in your own way to receiving greater? Many of us form beliefs when we are young and hold on to them with strong conviction. If our beliefs are challenged, we respond angrily because of their importance in our lives. But what if our beliefs are not working for us?

From a very young age, I was committed and convinced of my calling. Even though it evolved as I experienced different situations, it never wavered. If you do not gain a firm conviction over who you are and what you desire for yourself, you will continue to make decisions that will cost you your chance at stardom. When I decided to start sharing my dreams with others, they laughed and said it was impossible to achieve. Now, at that moment, I had 1 of 2 choices: allow them to talk me out of my dreams or use everything within me to prove them wrong. As I stated above, I was encouraged to get a job and live life. I mean, people wanted me to ignore my gifts as if they did not matter. Although having a high-paying job may sound nice to many, it did not excite me. Of course, it would pay the bills and keep me from being a little more than broke, but was I willing to settle for that? I gave myself permission to recreate my belief system and bet on myself. I gave myself the authority to be responsible for myself. I had to be true to the woman I wanted to become. Even with all of the naysayers, my truth would not allow me to participate in a belief I did not believe in.

As you continue on your life journey, remember that your beliefs are a choice. We have the power to choose our beliefs, as our beliefs become our reality. Before we close this chapter, let's look at the areas of your life where your limiting beliefs are holding you back:

- **Financially:** I will never get out of debt. Money does not grow on trees.
- **Relationships:** I am not loveable. I am not the kind of person who can commit. I cannot find my perfect match.
- **Physically:** Diets do not work for me. Eating healthy is too much work.
- **Emotionally:** I am moody. The healthiest way to deal with emotions is to let them all out as soon as they come up.
- **Mentally:** Only smart people can do great things. If you are too intelligent, people will not like you.

What is your payoff for clinging to those limiting beliefs? Your conscious mind may think about making changes, but your subconscious, where the habits have been etched, will keep pulling you into the same rut. Stop the vicious cycle and come out of the rut you are keeping yourself in. Get out of your head and into your life. I am rooting for you. Just remember, you CAN change your beliefs. When you change your beliefs, your thoughts will change, which will cause your actions to change. Different actions lead to different results.

Your Scriptures:

- Mark 11:22-24 — "Have faith in God," Jesus answered. "Truly I tell you, if anyone says to this mountain, 'Go, throw yourself into the sea,' and does not doubt in their heart but believes that what they say will happen, it will be done for them. Therefore I tell you, whatever you ask for in prayer, believe that you have received it, and it will be yours."
- John 20:31 — "But these are written so that you may believe that Jesus is the Christ, the Son of God, and that by believing you may have life in his name."
- Matthew 17:20 — "He said to them, 'Because of your little faith. For truly, I say to you, if you have faith like a grain of mustard seed, you will say to this mountain, 'Move from here to there,' and it will move, and nothing will be impossible for you."

The Message 108 Coaching Tips

Happiness. Using your gift will make you a much happier person because you will be doing what you love to do. You are also blessing others by using your gift, which increases your happiness and brings you blessings for being a blessing. I believe people would be much happier if they used the gifts that God gave them instead of going to work daily to perform duties that are not feeding their spirit.

Believe. You have to believe in your dream. If you don't, who will? You have to believe when you tell yourself it is possible. Do not quit. You must rest, but don't you quit. There is something deep inside all of us that we want to do. If you're going to make it a reality, do not give up. Believe, and don't quit.

Use it. Your current job may not be your dream job, but it's where you are presently. So, use your dream there. For example, I became a certified speech and debate teacher to use my gift while earning a living. My goal has always been to travel and motivate. Having young children, I could not do that, but I did not let that stop me from using my gift to motivate. In my mind, I had a captive audience every day for eight hours that I used my gift to encourage. In every situation and job you have, use your gifts. Be creative. Find a way to incorporate them into your daily life to where it becomes what you do.

CHARLOTTE CRUMLEY ARRINGTON

The Power of Manifestation

Have you ever heard someone say, "Act as if it is already?" When it comes to the power of manifesting, you are essentially acting based on a feeling that something is yours and making it real. When you manifest, you are making it known to the universe that this thing — whether a lifestyle or something materialistic — will be yours. How many of you use vision boards? You create a visual of the life you want to manifest. You get a piece of cardboard and magazine, then cut and glue pictures that relate to your vision for your future onto the cardboard. Once you finish, hang it somewhere you can see it daily. Each day, you will become more of what you see. You begin to envision yourself in a mansion, so you clean your apartment or home more thoroughly. You pretend your Toyota is a Mercedes, so you begin to take care of it better. How many of you are guilty of doing this? Do not leave me out here by myself. Or how about you carry a knock-off Prada bag, but can't nobody tell you it's not real. You know it is fake, but in your mind, it is the most expensive purse you own. When you manifest greater, you give yourself permission to see yourself in the life you want. It is almost like living within your dreams and getting a taste of your future before actually getting there.

When it comes to the power of manifestation, you must understand how manifesting works. Each thought creates an energy flow within and around your physical beings. Thus, your energy will attract its likeness. For example, if you think you suck, your energy will kind of…well, suck. However, when you think high-level thoughts, such as "I'm a winner," you will think, feel, and move like a winner. You will exude an energy of confidence and attract great experiences into your life. When it comes to manifesting, your thoughts will inform your energy, and your energy will manifest into your experiences. Your thoughts and energy create your reality. This is why your mood and energy need to be in sync with your beliefs, faith, and mindset. Your ability to create realities is also based on the purities within your mind, heart, and vibrations. For some, manifesting is how they get in alignment with God and his desires for them. For others, it is how they attract what they put out in the universe. Whichever route is your destiny, know that this concept requires you to do some serious soul searching and interior cleaning.

For me, I have become a master of this concept, as I have applied it to everything I have brought from the spiritual realm into my physical presence. If there is something I want, I go within my energy and mood and begin to give it life. I post pictures, pretend as if it was already, and envision it so I can see myself with what I desire. Before I had children, I always envisioned myself with twins, and when blessed with children, my first two were twins. When I was younger, I was infatuated with watching planes and imagined myself working on one, and I became a flight attendant. I can remember a time when all I saw was myself smiling and serving others. What I saw then is now my reality. It is almost like déjà vu. Everything I saw for myself, regardless if it was tangible or intangible, I have created in my reality. This is my life now, and what a beautiful sight it is.

I know you may be thinking this is a lot and who has time for this. Yes, this level of manifesting requires you to do some strange work, and many people may even look at you strangely. But you have to understand you will only attract what you manifest. So, if you think this is too much, you have already attracted the power of "remaining the same" because your energy tells the universe you are not willing to do the work. You did not come this far to remain in your comfort zone, did you? No? Good! Let us continue then.

As you do the work, remember manifesting can only be attracted through your feelings or energy. How you respond to the situation will send a vibration to the universe, giving it permission to create or deny your reality. The good about this is, it is never a one and done. You can elude good feelings today and begin manifesting. Or you can delay your journey until you are able to believe and feel that what you seek is real. When your primary function is to be happy, then whatever comes to you is irrelevant. Happiness is your true manifestation.

Since this concept may be new for many of you, allow me to offer you five key principles to assist you in manifesting. When practicing these principles, make sure to stay connected to the goal of feeling first and attracting second.

- Principle One: Clear Space
- Principle Two: Get Clear
- Principle Three: Think It, Feel It, Believe It!
- Principle Four: Chill!
- Principle Five: Know the Universe Has Your Back

Principle One: Clear Space

Before you begin the manifestation process, you must take the time to release all disbelief in your power to be happy. When it comes to manifesting, you must cleanse your energy and vibrations of any limiting beliefs that can stop you from committing to the process. Being open and willing to the universe gives God the power to grant your desires. Closed energy cannot receive greatness; thus, you must remove everything that stops you from being great. I help myself by going into prayer to seek guidance and the strength to focus on what is important rather than what I am familiar with. It is always easy to convert back to what we know when challenged. We must be stripped of our old selves in order to step into what is new.

Principle Two: Get Clear

Now that we have a clear space and have released all negative energy, it is time to clarify who we are and our intentions. Please understand, clarity is mandatory when it comes to manifesting your desires. You must be clear on what you want to call in. Otherwise, you can manifest a lot of what you do not want. Focus on what you desire, and then make a list of all that goes along with it. For example, if you are seeking to manifest a job you want, make a list of all the things about the job that make you happy, such as the office, the people, the salary, etc. Become specific and committed about what you want. This list helps you clarify your intentions and access a vibrant mental picture of what you desire.

When you get clear on how you want to feel, you can begin to access that feeling. That feeling is what makes the manifestation come into form. You can write a thousand lists and make a million vision boards, but if you do not clearly feel what you want to experience, it will never truly manifest into form.

Principle Three: Think It, Feel It, Believe It!

With our space now clear and our intentions pure, take the next few days to generate a feeling of what you want to achieve. You can access the feeling through meditation, visioning exercises, or doing a form of exercise you love. Let your thoughts execute the feeling, and let the feeling take over your energy. Think, feel, believe, and celebrate.

Principle Four: Chill!

To truly manifest your desires, you must chill out and pack your patience! Allow your commitment and faithfulness to guide you into believing that what you desire is on the way. Also, trust that God has a much better plan than you do. Though you are clear about what you want, you cannot control the timing or the form in which it comes.

Principle Five: Know the Universe Has Your Back

When you are in the know, you are deliberate about what you want. When you are in the know, you no longer vibrate energy of fear or disbelief. You just know. This process is healing and powerful, and it leads to a deep inner knowing that you are right where you need to be. Accepting your greatness in this moment, right now, is what manifests more greatness. When you feel it, you live it — regardless of what is happening on the outside. In time, the universe catches up with your energy, and your desires come into form.

Staying committed to this process, I know firsthand it is not the easiest as it requires a lot of patience and tons of faith. However, when what you manifest comes to fruition, you will be dancing in joy and ready to live the life you have worked so hard for. Now that you have the principles, it is time to get aligned and start your process. Use the principles above and fill out the following questions:

What beliefs do you need to remove to clear your energy and vibration so you can start your process?

_____
_____
_____
_____
_____
_____
_____
_____
_____
_____
_____
_____
_____

What are you manifesting in your life? List your desire and what comes along with it so the universe can prepare your table for you.

I am manifesting:

My manifestations include:

Now that you are cleansed and clear, how are you feeling? What energy methods are you doing to get your feelings going?

___

How is your patience? What are some ways you intend to enjoy the journey without reverting back to what is familiar to you?

Who do you have to support you on this journey? List everyone you can call as you do the work preparing and positioning yourself for what is about to come into your life.

THE MESSAGE 108

_____

_____

_____

_____

_____

_____

_____

_____

_____

_____

Remember that you attract what you believe. Therefore, make every effort to keep your internal vibration high and take care of yourself so you are in the best possible place to create desired change for yourself. Manifesting takes focus, time, and commitment, but it is so worth it when your dreams become your reality.

Your Scriptures:

- Proverbs 11:25 — "A generous man will prosper; he who refreshes others will himself be refreshed."
- Psalms 37:4 — "Delight yourself in the Lord and he will give you the desires of your heart."
- Luke 6:38 — "Give, and it will be given to you. A good measure, pressed down, shaken together

and running over, will be poured into your lap. For with the measure you use, it will be measured to you."

The Message 108 Coaching Tips

Visualize. You have to have a clear picture in your mind of what you want. You have to train yourself to take a few minutes every day to think about what you want and feel it. For example, as a motivational speaker, I often visualize myself walking on stage and giving a speech. I visualize my outfit. I visualize the audience, and I feel their emotions. At the end of my visualizing, I hear the applause and words of adoration from my audience. If it is a car you want, visualize yourself driving down the street in that car. Go to the dealership and test drive the vehicle you want. If it is a house you want, visualize the location of your home, how many rooms your home will have, etc. Then go and look at those houses. It does not matter if you have the money or not. Once you find your dream home, dream car, or whatever it is that your heart desires, you will have everything you need to make it a reality.

Believe. When you first start manifesting your dreams, it may seem weird at first, but all you have to do is believe the visions you see in your mind. The more time you spend visualizing what you want, the more real it becomes and the more focused you will be to obtain it. You have to believe you will get that house or car, or even that peace you want. If you are not hurting yourself or anyone else with your dreams, you can have whatever you want in this life. You just have to believe.

Time. Everything takes time. You must understand that things do not happen overnight. You have to put in the time and work it takes to make your vision a reality. When I am manifesting something, I am not just sitting back and daydreaming about it. I am putting in the work. For example, I wanted a new car. So, while I was visualizing myself driving that car and shopping for it even though I had no money in my pocket, I worked and saved up for it. When I first thought of the idea for this book, I would go to bookstores and imagine my book on the shelves. I did that for twenty years. Now when I go into the bookstore, I will finally see my book on the shelf. Twenty years is a long time, but that is okay. What matters is my dream became a reality, and all those days and nights I spent manifesting it have paid off.

Work. You have to do the work! There is no way around it. This goes back to studying your gift and doing what it takes to get it done. You have to do what it takes to have the things you are manifesting. If you dream of being a heart surgeon, you have to go to medical school. If you visualize yourself singing opera, you have to go to school and educate yourself in music. You are not going to manifest anything by just thinking about it. You have to do the work. People who are great at what they do did not only visualize it; they worked at it. You have to do the work. Sometimes, it is a quick turnaround; sometimes, it may take years. But it will happen. It is up to you, how much you want it, and your belief in miracles.

Congratulations

In the book *Abundance Now*, motivational speaker and best-selling author Lisa Nichols wrote, "I have nothing to hide! I have nothing to protect! I have nothing to prove! I have nothing to defend! Now, who do I choose to be?" *Who do I choose to be?* That question alone made me reconsider my "why." Understanding the relevance gave me the permission needed to accept who I was to become after the work was complete. Your "why" is vital to how you consistently work on yourself even after completing this book. Self-growth is a lifestyle. We are working toward breaking generational curses, self-sabotaging thoughts, disappointment, the pain inflicted by others, and projected fears that have suffocated our growth. We wonder why our lives are in turmoil, but look at everything we carry.

Today, we will give ourselves permission to live, especially since we did the work yesterday to forgive ourselves. Today, reward yourself by sharing your goals, visions, hopes and dreams, love, and prayer for the person you are now choosing to become. She deserves to know what is ahead of her so she can plan accordingly to receive it while being ready for any shifts life may bring. It is time to have what you always prayed for, what God ordained for you, and the ability to be grateful. See the good in what was intended for evil. Today, offer yourself the courage and permission to love yourself to no end. Go and have a great day on purpose. Get your hair and nails done; get a manicure and pedicure. Get a massage. Sign up for a gym membership. Have a lunch date alone at the most expensive restaurant without worrying about the prices on the menu. Today, it is about celebrating your present life and preparing for your life to come.

Allow today to be the start of your freedom. Get intentional about your next steps and prepare yourself mentally, emotionally, and physically for the journey. Because I am here to warn you that the devil is always at work and busy. Your happiness will insult him, thus making him monkey-wrench your plans by causing delays and detours. However, if you are prepared while executing your plans, his weapons will never gain power. They will just become steps to help during your elevation to reach your destination faster!

Here's to Manifesting & Achieving What Your Heart Desires. Cheers!

CHARLOTTE CRUMLEY ARRINGTON

About the Author

Charlotte Crumley Arrington is the mother of three phenomenal adult children Joseph, Jessica and Brian, a businesswoman, and a motivational speaker and life coach. She is very passionate about encouraging people to do what God has called them to do and teaching the tangible skills to make it happen. Charlotte's diverse background and experiences throughout her life have all prepared her for this fulfilling opportunity to motivate and coach with purpose. Charlotte has had the unique opportunity to travel worldwide, encouraging people to believe in the beauty of their dreams.

Charlotte was born in Honolulu, Hawaii, and raised in San Diego California, by two Amazing parents Barbara and Jesse Crumley. She has an older brother Duvall and sister Latarsha. Charlotte comes from a family of Believers. Charlotte's grandfather, Reverend Willis

Brown, Sr., is the founder of Gethsemane Baptist Church in Charleston, South Carolina, which has been in her family for 112 years and is now being pastored by her first cousin Reverend Herbert Harvey. After high school, Charlotte enrolled in Howard University in Washington DC, where she studied and received her BA in Speech Communications. During her time at Howard, Charlotte married Recording Artist Joe Tex, Jr. After graduating, Charlotte furthered her education by becoming a certified speech and debate teacher.

Charlotte had no idea she would use her communication and speaking gifts thousands of feet in the air amongst some of the world's most influential people. Charlotte's first dream had always been to become a flight attendant, and it wasn't long before that dream came true. She became a first-class flight attendant with American Airlines and continued with Swift Aviation, a private charter airline, as a lead flight attendant. While working with the private jet company, Charlotte served the White House Press Corps, NBA, NHL, MLB, MLS, A-list celebrities, and presidents and dignitaries of other countries.

Charlotte has also served as the opening act for several comedy shows, starring Steve Harvey, Dave Chappelle, and Tommy Davidson. Charlotte has had the distinct honor of serving as the keynote speaker for an American Airlines flight attendant graduation, Conoco Petroleum in Houston, Texas, and Bradford Business College, also in Houston. Charlotte has also worked with the NBA, NHL MLB as a motivator.

Currently, Charlotte works as a patient access advocate trainer for a bio-medical marketing firm in La Jolla, California. While Charlotte's accomplishments are numerous, she has also realized her first calling and career in ministry, beginning in 2000 under the leadership of Dr. Ralph Douglas West at the Church Without Walls in Houston, Texas, where she served as a youth and women's pastor. She currently attends The Heart Revolution Church in San Diego.

Charlotte is now focusing on her mission, passion, and purpose of motivating people to reach their highest potential and follow their dreams — just as she is doing, too. Her Mission is for people to achieve their dreams and manifest their hearts desires.